GEOGRAPHICAL ORIGIN OF GERMAN IMMI-GRATION TO WISCONSIN

BY

KATE EVEREST LEVI, PH. D.

[From Wisconsin Historical Collections, Vol. XIV]

MADISON
STATE HISTORICAL SOCIETY OF WISCONSIN
1898

GEOGRAPHICAL ORIGIN OF GERMAN IMMIGRATION TO WISCONSIN.

BY KATE EVEREST LEVI, PH. D.[1]

NORTHEASTERN GERMANY.

EDUCATION AND RELIGION.

In education, the northern provinces of Germany differ considerably. The percentages of illiterate recruits in 1882 and 1883, in these several provinces, were as follows: Mecklenburg Schwerin 0.56, Mecklenburg Strelitz 0, Pomerania 0.82, East Prussia 5.5, West Prussia 7.97, Posen 9.75.

Where the population is of German stock, or has been Germanized, as in Mecklenburg, Brandenburg, Pomerania, and East Prussia, the inhabitants belong almost exclusively to the Lutheran faith. West Prussia and Posen were long dominated by Poland, and bear traces of that influence in both language and religion. West Prussia and Silesia are

---

[1] In *Wis. Hist. Colls.*, xii, we published a valuable paper on "How Wisconsin Came by its Large German Element," by Kate Asaphine Everest (now Mrs. Kate Everest Levi). In *Trans. Wis. Acad. Sci., Arts and Letters*, viii, there is contained another article by the same author, entitled "Early Lutheran Immigration to Wisconsin." The present paper is a further study of German settlement in this State, with especial reference to the localities in Germany from which the several groups came. As the conditions under which this paper was prepared were identical with those of its predecessors, the reader is referred to the author's prefatory note, in *Wis. Hist. Colls.*, xii, p. 299. The statistics of population in Wisconsin, herein cited, are, unless otherwise noted, from the federal census of 1890.— ED.

about equally divided between the German Protestant and Polish Catholic elements, while in Posen the latter prevails. As in other matters, the Baltic peoples are conservative in religion. While they exhibit a strong theological bias, and numerous shades of doctrine have sprung up among them, they are yet very loyal to the Lutheran church. It was here, as we shall see, that opposition to religious innovations led to persecution and emigration.

CHARACTERISTICS.

The North German, in contrast to the South German, is tall, slender, well-proportioned, light-complexioned, and has features not clearly outlined. Of this type, the mental characteristics are various.

"In the Mark beyond the Elbe, from the ground stock of the Low Saxon conquerors," says Treitschke,[1] "from emigrants of all German lands and from small fragments of the old Wendish settlers, a new German race has sprung up, hard and steadfast, steeled through hard labor on a scanty soil and through unremitting struggles with their neighbors, keen and independent after the manner of colonists, accustomed to look down on their Slavic neighbors, and as rugged and sharp (*schneidig*) as the good-humored, joking roughness of the low-German character permits." The result of this mixture of races in Brandenburg, is a most stirring, aggressive people, scarcely equalled in any portion of Germany.

The East Prussians, who are likewise composed of many different elements, possess to some extent the same progressive character.

Except the East Prussians, the Baltic peoples lack in aggressiveness. They are slow to adopt new ideas, cautious, but persevering. In the army the Pomeranian, who is a good type of this class, is regarded as one of the best of soldiers. His excellence does not consist in force of attack, but in extreme persistence. The Pomeranian possesses

---

[1] *Staaten Geschichte der Neuesten Zeit*, i, p. 25.

great seriousness, is sparing of words, clings steadfastly to old customs, and is zealous for his rights.[1] The Mecklenburgers are a strong, healthy race, homely, true-hearted, and not easily accessible to moral corruption.[2] Both of these peoples are among the best of farmers.

RELIGIOUS COLONIES.

As the Puritan colonies on the Atlantic shores were formed by immigrants in search of religious freedom, so the North German immigrants who came to Wisconsin in the years 1839 and 1843–45, left the " Fatherland " to escape persecution, and to establish communities in the New World where they might exercise their religion without restraint. The emigration that followed, was about the beginning of the emigration from North-eastern Germany, not only to Wisconsin but to America.

This religious persecution was due to a desire for union among Protestants. From the early years of the Reformation, there had existed in Germany two forms of the Protestant faith — the Lutheran, and Reformed or Calvinistic. The latter had its stronghold in South Germany, while Lutheranism was prevalent in the north. To the close of the seventeenth century, the lines between the two had been closely drawn; but from that time, modifications of dogmatic principles were gradually effected by means of Pietism and Rationalism. Doctrine became subordinate to "inner light" and to practical piety. The old antagonism became more and more incomprehensible to the new race. Rationalism was above dogmatic strife, and Pietism regarded the eternal love as the essence of Christianity. Hence the idea naturally arose that Protestantism might well return to its early unity. Among the advocates of this idea were Frederick I. and Frederick William I. of Prussia, who effected some minor changes. In this century, Schleiermacher became its spokesman, and Frederick

---

[1] Steinhard, *Deutschland und Sein Volk*, ii, p. 714.
[2] *Ibid.*, p. 735.

William III. its propagator, though they differed materially
as to the manner in which it was to be carried out.

The year 1817 marks the beginning of a new epoch in religious matters. In that year, Claus Harnes published his
ninety-five theses against rationalistic apostasy; and in the
same year, at the three hundredth anniversary of the Reformation, King Frederick William III. of Prussia proclaimed the union of the Reformed and Lutheran churches.
The great point of difference between the two creeds lay
in the doctrine of the Lord's Supper; the Lutherans taught
the real presence of Christ's body "in," "with," and
"under" the bread and wine of the sacrament; the Calvin-
ists made these symbolic of the real spiritual presence to
believers only. Other points of difference related to the
doctrine of predestination, which Luther had not taught in
any strict sense; but the Reformed church laid great em-
phasis on moral character, and for that reason was more
inclined to the idea of unity than the Lutherans, who em-
phasized doctrinal points.

To the king, who was of the Reformed faith, the union
seemed most simple. "According to my' opinion," he had
said, "the communion strife is only an unfruitful theological subtlety, of no account in comparison with the funda-
mental faith of the Scriptures."[1] The fact that he was outside of the church to which the great majority of his people belonged, was a source of great regret to him. Though
the act was performed by the king in the profound belief
that he was called to do that work, yet his unfortunate belief in the sacred prerogative of kings, which led him to
carry it out in a thoroughly absolute manner, was destined
to call forth an opposition which ended in the partial failure of the attempt. The union was proclaimed without
the consent of the churches; in 1822, a new *agende* was
drawn up by Bishop Eylert and the court theologians, and
in 1830 was rigidly enforced. Schleiermacher, the upholder
and defender of the Union, was strongly opposed to the

[1] Treitschke, ii, p. 240.

agende, partly on account of its source, which was the royal will instead of the free choice of the church; partly on account of its contents, on the ground that they were antiquated and reactionary.

While the movement had many warm supporters, and was imitated by other German courts,—Baden, Nassau, and the Palatinate of the Rhine,—yet it was not heartily supported by the rationalistic element, and on the other hand aroused a new Lutheran consciousness. It was taken as an attempt to root out Lutheranism, which the revival of Germany's great past was more likely to restore. This was especially the case in those parts of Prussia where Lutheranism existed almost unmixed —where there was no sympathy with Reformed doctrines, and the union was not felt as a practical necessity. This was the case in North Germany — Saxony, Mecklenburg, and Pomerania.

For some years the opposition was confined to literary polemics,[1] but in 1830, when the new *agende* was enforced by cabinet orders, Prof. Scheibel of Breslau founded a separate society of two or three hundred families, and, being refused permission to worship according to the old *agende*, left the country. Many Silesian pastors followed his example, and resistance spread rapidly to Erfurt, Magdeburg, and different parts of Pomerania. At Erfurt, the leader of the movement, and afterwards of the emigration to America, was Rev. Johannes A. A. Grabau, pastor of the Evangelical church. In spite of an early education under the influence of a pastor of the United faith, Grabau seems to have kept his preference for the Lutheran church. Finally, in 1836, he reached the conclusion that the Union was contrary to the Scriptures, and declared publicly that he could no longer use the new *agende* with good conscience. His society agreed with him, and when he was suspended from his office and a new pastor put in charge, they followed him to his house, where services were held. This, too, was forbidden, but they decided "to obey God rather

---

[1] Schaff-Herzog, *Encyclopedia of Religious Knowledge*, ii, p. 1376.

than man." The separate society grew until it reached a membership of nearly four hundred.

Meanwhile, at Magdeburg, another small body of Lutherans had separated from the Union church, and were holding services at the home of a captain of the guards, Henry von Rohr. The movement was spreading in Pomerania, and many pastors and laymen were being persecuted. In 1837, Grabau was imprisoned, and, at that time, there were said to be twenty pastors in prison or banished.[1] Laymen who refused to send their children to the United schools, or who availed themselves of the administration of Lutheran pastors in baptism or marriage ceremonies, but especially those who refused to pay the taxes required for the support of a pastor of the United faith, were imprisoned, fined, or otherwise punished.

At length von Rohr, who had been deprived of his position as captain of the guards, for his refusal to conform, assisted Grabau to escape from prison, where, it was claimed, he was illegally detained. They reached Seehof, on the coast of Pomerania, in safety. Previous to this time, frequent calls had come to Grabau from the Pomeranian churches which had been deprived of their pastors, and he now visited and conducted services in the different societies. Already the question of emigration had been talked of, and letters were received from friends in Ohio. The life of Grabau, written by his son, from which I have obtained the facts of his personal experience, states that Grabau advised them to wait until it was definitely settled whether the Lutheran faith would be tolerated. Accordingly, letters were sent to the government asking, in case it should not be tolerated, for permission to emigrate. To the first question the answer was, "The Lutheran church is within the United church; and outside of it, the king will tolerate no Lutheran church in this land." It is further stated that permission was given to emigrate, in case they proved to the satisfaction of the government that they had

[1] *Lebenslauf des Ehrwurdigen J. A. A. Grabau von John A. Grabau*, p. 26.

a pastor, but not otherwise. In consequence of this, many societies in Pomerania and the one at Magdeburg, placed themselves in communication with Grabau, asking him to become their pastor. Grabau, meanwhile, had been imprisoned a second time, but finally he received permission to emigrate.

This was the spring of 1839, and, with Magdeburg as a center, a large emigration was arranged for that year. Captain von Rohr was chosen to engage passage for the company, and to go in advance to America and select places for settlement. He decided on Buffalo and Milwaukee. Just why he selected Wisconsin, it is impossible to say; but after traveling through New York, Ohio, Illinois, and Wisconsin, in order to find the best possible location for a settlement, Wisconsin and New York seemed to him the most favorable. It is thought that the considerations of cheap lands, forests, good soil, and temperate climate, influenced him.[1]

To defray the expenses of the journey, a common treasury was formed, to which the wealthier members contributed part of their means to assist the poor to accompany them. Directors were appointed for each company, to take charge of the money and distribute it according to the needs of the poorer people.

Passage was engaged for a thousand people, in five American sailing vessels. Rev. E. F. L. Krause, a pastor from Silesia, with his society accompanied them. They emigrated in the latter part of July, and reached Buffalo, October 5. Captain von Rohr had met them in New York, and told them of the places he had chosen, and their advantages. Accordingly about half of them settled in and near Buffalo, while the remainder came to Wisconsin with von Rohr.

The latter were chiefly Pomeranians. It is doubtless this body of immigrants that is mentioned in Buck's *Pioneer History of Milwaukee*. "The year 1839," he says,

---

[1] See author's article in *Wis. Hist. Colls.*, xii, pp. 330 and elsewhere.-ED.

"brought the first installment of immigrants from Germany and Norway. The effect of their arrival, with their gold and silver wherewith to purchase land, was electric. * * * Whereas Milwaukee had been under financial depression before, now all doubts about the future were dissipated." Again, he says: "The first German colony arrived in 1839. It consisted of about eight hundred men, women and children [the number is probably exaggerated]. They brought with them the necessary housekeeping utensils and encamped on the lake shore south of Huron street. The men went about in a business way, examined the government plats in the land office, and having ascertained by all means in their power where lands well-timbered and watered could be purchased, they entered lands bounding on the Milwaukee River, between Milwaukee and Washington (later Ozaukee) counties. A small number remained in the village [of Milwaukee], but the most of them employed themselves without delay in clearing and cultivating lands. The men immediately declared their intention of becoming American citizens, every man signing his name to his petition, to the number of seventy in one day."[1]

The majority of the immigrants, over three hundred people, and probably those still possessing some means, went to Mequon, and there formed the Freistadt colony, a name chosen, no doubt, to commemorate their new freedom; some also settled in Cedarburg, while a few remained in Milwaukee.[2]

These settlers were from Pomerania, chiefly from the farming district of Stettin, on the Oder, and from the neighborhood of Camin and Greifenberg, on the Baltic. The Wisconsin settlers were chiefly farm laborers and handicraftsmen, and, accordingly, well adapted to pioneer life. They bought nearly all of the western half of the town of Mequon, where they built log houses and improved the land.

---

[1] P. 181; and an address by Judge Miller, p. 265.

[2] Adolph A. Koss, *Milwaukee*, p. 103. Anton Eickhoff, *In der Neuen Heimath*, p. 372.

Captain von Rohr had come with them, and during the first year he conducted their services until the arrival from Buffalo of Rev. E. F. L. Krause, who was their first pastor; immediately on his arrival, a log church was built.

In the Milwaukee society, services were held in a house built by a fisherman on land near Chestnut street, given him by Byron Kilbourn. It was a solid structure, built after the German fashion of panel work and clay filling. They had no pastor, but the school teacher held services, while Krause came occasionally from Freistadt.[1]

In 1843, another large immigration followed from Pomerania, from the district of Stettin, and the neighborhood of Colberg, Treptow, and Camin, on the Baltic; also from Brandenburg, from the country lying between Cüstrin and Wrietzen, on the Oder. Rev. G. A. Kindermann acted as their leader. He had been directed to the Pomeranian churches by Grabau, during the earlier period of the persecution. Others continued to come until 1845. It was the reports of the earlier emigrants, who were their friends and acquaintances, that led them to Wisconsin.

The cause of this emigration also, was religious persecution, which had not yet ceased, though it was abating.[2] But there were, also, other causes. Differences had sprung up in the Lutheran church in Germany, over the question of church government. The decrees of the synod were, that in disputed questions of doctrine the majority of votes should decide. Against this, one party protested and claimed that the only ultimate authority was the Scriptures. To this party, which was the weaker, Kindermann belonged. To avoid unpleasantness, therefore, they decided to emigrate with those of like mind.

This company likewise formed a common treasury to which the wealthier members contributed from fifteen to twenty per cent of their means to assist the poor, both in the passage over and in purchasing land. It was expected

---

[1] Koss, p. 103.

[2] Separate worship was allowed by King William IV., in 1846.

that the money would be returned with interest, but in many cases this was never done. Of these immigrants, some remained in Milwaukee and joined the first settlers in the neighborhood of Chestnut street, but the majority went to the farms. Kirchhayn, Washington county, and Lebanon, Dodge county, with Ixonia, Jefferson county, were chosen for settlement. The settlers in Washington county were from the Baltic regions,— Camin, Colberg and Treptow, — while those from Stettin and the *Oderbrüche*, between 70 and 100 families, settled at Lebanon and Ixonia. A committee had been sent by the latter people to Sauk county, but they were not pleased with the country and returned to the Rock River. The meadows along the Rock River reminded them of their home in the *Oderbrüche*, and were speedily chosen. These settlers were descendants of the colonists whom Frederick the Great had settled in Brandenburg. They were independent proprietors in Germany, and a refined and intelligent class; they are still distinguished for those qualities, among the North Germans in that part of Wisconsin. Even where they have not as much means as their neighbors, their style of living is higher. The land in Lebanon and Ixonia being more open and easier to cultivate than that in Washington county, the settlers in the former districts had fewer difficulties to encounter, and obtained success more easily.

Between 1850 and 1860, a number of the early settlers sold out and went from Freistadt, Cedarburg, and Kirchhayn to Sherman, Sheboygan county, and Cooperstown, Manitowoc county, where land was in greater abundance.

The large Pomeranian and North German element in Wisconsin is undoubtedly due in great measure to this first body of immigrants. Through their reports to friends and relatives in the "Fatherland," many have since followed them, and either joined the original communities or passed into the northern counties where land was more abundant. Another potent influence was a tour through North Germany, made in 1853 by Rev. Johannes Grabau and Captain von Rohr. By their conversations and reports about the success of their countrymen in Wisconsin, they caused many Lutherans to settle here. Emigration from the northern countries had scarcely begun at that period; but since 1870, Pomerania, Prussia, and the adjoining countries have furnished the greater part of the German emigration, of which Wisconsin has received a large share.

LATER IMMIGRATION.

There are, in Wisconsin, six large groups from North-eastern Germany: (1) The Milwaukee, Ozaukee, and Washington county group; (2) in Dodge and Jefferson counties, with Watertown as a center; (3) Manitowoc and Sheboygan counties; (4) the northern townships of Winnebago county, with the neighboring townships of Waushara, Waupaca, and Outagamie counties; (5) the south-central townships of Shawano county, with some small groups in northern Waupaca county; (6) the north-central towns of Marathon county, and the southern portion of Lincoln county. Smaller groups are also found in Fond du Lac county; Green Lake and Marquette counties; Columbia and Sauk counties; Vernon, Sauk, and Juneau counties, about Wonewoc and Elroy; Buffalo and La Crosse counties; and in the cities of Milwaukee, Oshkosh, Portage, and Fond du Lac.

The *nuclei* of the first two groups were formed between 1839 and 1846 by the Old Lutherans whose settlement has just been described. From 1854 to 1860, another large body immigrated and either joined the original settlements, or settled in the north-eastern towns of Dodge county, in Sheboygan and Manitowoc counties, in the northern part of Fond du Lac county, and in Green Lake county, while a few individuals went into the northern counties before 1860. Since 1848, they have continued to come in large numbers every year until the present time; but their immigration to the State was especially large from 1854 to 1857, in 1866, and just after the Franco-Prussian war. Since the two organized bodies of immigrants,—of 1839 and 1843,—the North German settlers, with few excep-

tions, have come by private enterprise, either singly, or in
groups of two or three families. They first joined their
friends and relatives already located here, worked some-
times in the same locality for a period, and then left for
less-accessible portions of the State, where land was
cheaper.

In Milwaukee, there is a large North German element,
chiefly Pomeranians and Mecklenburgers. They belong to
twenty-three Lutheran congregations, the majority of which
are situated on the north and west sides of the city.[1]
They aggregate seven thousand voting members, or between twenty and thirty thousand people, belonging chiefly
to the laboring classes. These people brought little means
with them. One of the early American settlers, who owned
land and had frequent dealings with the Germans, says
that when they purchased land they often paid not more
than five dollars down, yet he never took a lot back. They
are employed in the mills and factories, and in various
trades; most of them own their homes; it is a community
well worth study, in many respects. The air of thrift is
very noticeable. The people cannot be said to exhibit
great public spirit, nor unusual business enterprise; but
while there is no pretense of display, there is evidence of
genuine comfort and well-being.

Between 1850 and 1865, Watertown[2] and the towns of
Herman, Theresa, Lomira, and Portland in Dodge county,
and Ixonia, Waterloo, Lake Mills, Aztalan, Farmington,
Jefferson, and Hebron in Jefferson county, received the

---

[1] There are six congregations on the south side of the city.

[2] Watertown increased in population from about 1,800 to 10,000 between
the years 1845 and 1868, the German element preponderating. In the fifth
ward there is a large settlement of Mecklenburgers who came between 1854
and 1860. Three Lutheran societies and one Moravian, contain between
700 and 750 families, of whom the majority came in the same period.
Besides the Mecklenburgers and a few people from Brandenburg, the rest,
who form the larger part, are from Pomerania; in one church is a group
from the circle of Pridlaw; in another, are people from Stettin, Colberg,
and Camin.

greater part of their North German population.[1] In those towns, the Pomeranian element predominates, especially in Herman, Lomira, Theresa, Farmington, Lake Mills, and Waterloo. The remainder are from the two Mecklenburgs, Brandenburg, and a few from West Prussia.

Since 1865, many of the adjoining towns have been filling up with North Germans — new arrivals, or sons of the earlier immigrants. They have taken the place of the early American, Irish, or Norwegian settlers; such towns are Hustisford and Hubbard, first settled by Americans; Emmet, Richwood, Reeseville, and Clyman, in Dodge county, where Germans have taken the place of the Irish population; Ashippun, in the same county, where the early Norwegian settlers have within ten years been superseded by North Germans. In Waukesha county, the original Norwegian element has gone to the Red River valley, and Germans are taking their places; the census of 1890 shows the proportion of German-born to be 16.9 per cent of the

---

[1] The Pomeranians in Herman came from the districts of Stargard, Regenwalde, Dramburg, and Schiefelbein (the central part of farther Pomerania). The immigration occurred between the years 1847 and 1860, but chiefly from 1848 to 1855. In Theresa and Lomira, the population consists mainly of Germans from the northeastern provinces. Among the Germans in Lomira and Theresa, are sixty or seventy families from the districts of Colberg and Treptow, Pomerania; and twenty families from Mecklenburg Schwerin, who settled there between 1854 and 1868. In the adjoining towns, are people from the same duchy, who came in the same period. Between 1850 and 1860, a body of Brandenburgers settled in the two townships: one Lutheran congregation is composed of these people. Another congregation has 180 families of Pomeranians, Brandenburgers, and a few Mecklenburgers, who are located in these towns and in Hustisford, Clyman, Hubbard, and Lebanon. In Waterloo and Lake Mills, with Deerfield, Dane county, there are over a hundred families from Pomerania, who settled there between 1850 and 1870, in part superseding American settlers.

Farmington is settled almost exclusively with Pomeranians, but with them are a few Brandenburgers. Here also the German settlement began as early as 1854. Aztalan, Jefferson, and Hebron have, besides a large number of Germans from Bavaria, nearly a hundred families from Pomerania, West Prussia, and Mecklenburg. Here the majority settled between 1850 and 1860.

23

population of the county, an increase of 1.264, or 23 per cent since 1880.

The Pomeranian group in Herman were farm laborers (probably contract laborers) and peasants — about one-half, it is said, had owned some property in Germany. They purchased government farms of 80 acres each. Many have since enlarged their tracts, some of their neighbors having gone west, and now own farms of from 100 to 400 acres. The groups from Mecklenburg Schwerin were day-laborers, while the remaining groups were peasants, day-laborers, and handicraftsmen.

Beginning about 1854, North Germans, chiefly from Mecklenburg and Pomerania, and a few from Posen, formed comparatively large settlements in the towns of Leeds and Portage, and about Kilbourn, and scattered settlements in the towns of Columbus, Randolph, and Cambria.[1]

Passing north, we find that 25 per cent of the population of Green Lake county are German-born, and that chiefly North German. In 1848, the year that the first steamboat passed up Fox river to Princeton, the first Germans, six in number, settled in the county between Princeton and Berlin. From then to 1856, a few Germans came into the same region; but between 1856 and 1866, a large North German element, chiefly from Pomerania and Posen, settled near Princeton. One of their countrymen, August Theil, a blacksmith, located in Princeton, bought up farm lands, and sold them on credit to the immigrants. The Pomeranians located southeast of Princeton, where there are about 225 families — Methodists and Lutherans; and west of Princeton, people from Posen — Protestants and Catholics — have a large settlement. In the towns of Manchester, Kingston, and Marquette there are Germans from Posen and the Neumark (northeastern portion of Brandenburg), together with Pomeranians and Mecklen-

---

[1] The Germans in Leeds are chiefly Mecklenburgers, those in Portage are from Pomerania and Posen, and about Kilbourn there are many Pomeranians.

burgers, who located there mainly in the years following the Franco-Prussian war.

The Germans in Fond du Lac county are chiefly from Rhenish Prussia, but the population of Eldorado and Friendship are about one-half Germans who came from the region of Naugard, Pomerania, from Prussia, and Mecklenburg, and settled first along the ridge road, attracted partly by the timber land. The majority came in 1855; since then, a few families have arrived in each year. In the city of Fond du Lac, there is a congregation of nearly 250 North German families, from Brandenburg chiefly, but also from Pomerania, Mecklenburg, Hanover, and Prussia. They came chiefly between 1860 and 1870, to work in Meyer's sash, door, and blind factory. Now they are employed in the tannery, and the yeast and furniture factories.

Sheboygan and Manitowoc counties are interesting because of the heterogeneous nature of their German population, though the majority in both counties is North German. Sheboygan contains 25.3 per cent, and Manitowoc 21.3 per cent German-born; the former shows a decided increase since 1880 — the latter, however, has decreased somewhat in the same period. The attraction in Sheboygan county has probably been the rapid growth of the manufacturing city of Sheboygan.

It is estimated that there are about 15,000 North Germans in Sheboygan county, settled chiefly in the towns of Mosel, Herman, Sheboygan, Plymouth, Greenbush, and Mitchell, while scattered settlements are found in the southern townships. One of the largest groups from any single province is a body of Brandenburgers, from the Uckermark, located in the southern part of Herman.[1] The North Germans followed the immigrants from South and Middle Germany. From 1850 to 1855, the population of the county increased from 8,379 to 20,391.

---

[1] In Mosel, there are some Pomeranians. The town of Sheboygan, and the eastern part of Plymouth, contain a large group of Pomeranians. On the western line of Plymouth, extending into the towns of Greenbush and Mitchell, are many Mecklenburgers.

In 1846, the population of Manitowoc county was said to be 629. In 1850 it was 3,702, and in 1860 about 28,000, among whom was a large proportion of Germans. Probably the first group of North Germans to settle in the county, were a body of men from Holstein, whom Frederick Burchhardt, a native of Saxony, met in Detroit and induced to go to Neshoto, where there was a saw-mill belonging to the Stringham Company, by whom he was employed. Some of the people located in Neshoto, others in Mishicott. This was about 1840. The next German settlers were mostly from Saxony and Rhenish Prussia. Between 1848 and 1865, a large number of Mecklenburgers and Pomeranians located in the county. There are said to be about 5,000 families of this class, together with the Hanoverians and Oldenburgers, who are known as Mecklenburgers from the fact that the majority came from Mecklenburg-Schwerin. These people belong to eleven or more Lutheran congregations.[1]

Passing to Winnebago county, we find the German element outside of Oshkosh, mostly confined to the northern towns. In the city of Oshkosh there are over 1,000 North German families, of which the men chiefly work in the lumber mills and factories, while a few are engaged in some independent business. They belong to four Lutheran churches and one German Methodist; of these, about 700 families are said to be from Pomerania, — the rest come from Posen, Mecklenburg, and East and West Prussia. The time of settlement is difficult to determine exactly, though it seems that few came before 1854, and the great bulk had settled in Oshkosh before 1870.

In Neenah, there is a group of one hundred families from the district of Stettin, Pomerania. The process of settlement began about 1865, and has continued to within five years. In the city and town of Neenah, and in the neigh-

---

[1] The location is, so far as I can learn, about as follows: The town of Maple Grove, and the adjoining towns of Cato, Franklin, and Rockland contain about 80 or 100 Pomeranian families; in Reedsville, there are a number of West Prussians, while in the city of Manitowoc, and scattered through the country, are the Mecklenburgers and Hanoverians.

boring towns of Clayton, Winnebago county, and Greenville, Outagamie county, there is a group of Mecklenburgers from the region of Krivitz, who now number with their families about 200 people. They are engaged in farming and various kinds of business, and are people of enterprise and intelligence.[1]

The navigation up the Wolf River, and the saw mills constructed along its banks, were the special influences that attracted this extensive German settlement, as well as the one farther north; but individuals have played some part as steamship agents, or by their business dealings.[2]

The settlements in the northern towns of Waupaca county and in Shawano county, which form the fifth group, were of a later growth. North of the Wolf River, the northeastern part of Waupaca county is heavily timbered; together with the eastern part of Shawano county, it was settled in the sixties. Over one-half of the population of Shawano county is German, of whom the most are from Pomerania, Mecklenburg, and Brandenburg. Grant and Washington,[3] Germania and Almon, are almost exclusively

[1] One of the first settlers was Frederick Krueger. In 1850, he, with four others,— one a Pomeranian,— bought 480 acres of land in Clayton. Neenah was then a more accessible market than Appleton, and settlement to the north and west had scarcely begun. In 1851 he returned to Krívitz, where his father was a wagon-maker. He married there, and soon after returned to America, accompanied by a large number from Krivitz and vicinity, perhaps 160 or 170 altogether. Eighteen or twenty of these followed him to Wisconsin, where the majority worked in the pineries, only three having sufficient means to buy land. Between 1850 and 1860, others followed and settled in Clayton, Greenville, and Neenah. Eleven of the original families were from Krivitz; among them was one man of considerable means.

[2] William Spiegelberg was for many years agent of the Hamburg-American Packet Company. Andrew Mertin, in Wolf River, was well known and influential among the Germans; and Peter Faust, a later settler, sent immigration pamphlets to Germany.

[3] Grant contains 210 Pomeranians and Mecklenburgers, and Washington 200 Pomeranians. In Herman, there are twelve Pomeranian families from the circle of Regenwalde, in the district of Stettin, who followed the Wolf River immigrants. In the city of Shawano, there are about 750 Germans in a population of 1,500.

German; while Holland, Pella, and Herman are three-fourths German.

The towns of Clayton, Winneconne, Winchester, and Wolf River, Winnebago county; Bloomfield, Waushara county; Fremont, Caledonia, Weyauwega, Saxeville, and Lind, Waupaca county; and, to a less extent, Dale, Ellington, Hortonia, Center, and Greenville, Outagamie county, contain a large North German population. Of these towns, Wolf River and Bloomfield are settled almost exclusively by North Germans from the district of Stettin, Pomerania, Posen, and East and West Prussia.[1] The so-called "Rat River settlement," east of the Wolf River, was started about 1854.[2] It gradually spread eastward, and now includes about 150 families, of whom three-fourths are from Pomerania, and one-fourth from Posen. West of Wolf River, about Orihula, the first Germans were from Rhenish Prussia, and located there in 1849 and 1850; but the great mass of North Germans in this region came between 1857 and 1865. They bought in succession government, Fox River, and railroad land.

It is said that seventy-five per cent of the population of Marathon county is of German parentage, and that chiefly *Platt Deutsch.* The largest group from one province are the Pomeranians, of whom there are from 1,000 to 1,500 families. There are many also from West Prussia and

---

[1] In Winchester, there are about 48 families from the district of Stettin,—mostly from the circles of Naugard and Regenwalde,—and 18 families from the district of Bromberg, Posen.

Of a population of 909 in Wolf River, about one-sixth are from Pomerania; of the rest, all but about 25 Americans, are mainly from East and West Prussia, and Posen. In Bloomfield, there are 80 Pomeranian families from the district of Stettin, circle of Randow, and 60 from the province of Posen.

[2] In 1854, William Spiegelberg, then a subordinate officer in the Prussian army, sent his father, three brothers, and two sisters to Wolf River, and he followed in 1857. They were from the circle of Regenwalde, district of Stettin. Their immigration, according to his own statement, was well known in the districts from which they came, and many followed him, settling in Winnebago, Shawano, and Lincoln counties.

Posen, and perhaps 150 families from Brandenburg. They are located in the northern and central towns chiefly — Marathon, Cassel, Maine, Berlin, Wein, Wausau, Stettin, Rib Falls, and Hamburg, which are solidly German. Some scattered settlements are found in the eastern townships, — Elderon, Pike Lake, Harrison, Easton, and Norrie. The western towns are more thickly settled, but the population there is mixed, though the North German element is large. German settlement began in 1855, in the towns of Maine and Berlin. Wausau (then known as Big Bull Falls) was a small place, possessing a saw and grist mill. A few Silesian families first settled in the town of Berlin; also, about the same time, a Pomeranian, August Kopplin, from Princeton. Finding an abundance of cheap land he wrote home to his relatives in Germany, urging them to come; many came and worked in the southern counties until they obtained means enough to purchase government land in the north, at $1.25 an acre. By 1858, as many as forty families were settled in the central towns. The first settlers entered the county by a trail. In 1857, they constructed a rough road by chopping down the trees; but for some time they were obliged to carry their grain 60 miles to Plover to be ground, or to grind it by hand. It took ten years to break 40 acres of land, no harvest could be raised for the first three or four years, and until 1861 wages were only fifty cents a day. The young men hired themselves out during the harvesting season in the southern counties, bringing home their wages. In 1867, a large body of Pomeranians arrived. August Kickbush, a store-keeper in Wausau, had that year returned to Pomerania, collected a large number of persons from Greifenberg and Regenwalde, — peasants and day-laborers, — and conducted them to Wisconsin. He states that his party consisted of 702 persons, including the children, but only a portion settled in Marathon county. By 1867, there were 700 German voters in the county, and 1,000 German families.

Another agency in the settlement of Marathon county was the Wisconsin Valley railway, which was constructed in 1874. The company owned 200,000 acres of land in Marathon and Lincoln counties. To induce immigration, they sent out pamphlets and maps through Wisconsin and Germany, and at one time had an agent traveling in Germany. The conditions of purchase were, that the timber should not be cut off until the land was paid for, or, if cut off, the proceeds should go toward paying for the land. Prices ranged from $2.50 to $8 an acre, according to quality and location. In every case, the Germans preferred hard-wood land.

The settlement of Lincoln county was similar to that of the central towns of Marathon county, though I have learned few details. Among the German settlers at Merrill, are sixteen families from Regenwalde and Naugard, in the district of Stettin. The census of 1890 shows 17.9 per cent of German-born, an increase from 359 to 2,151, since 1880.

Settlement in the western townships began in 1879, through the agency of a Milwaukee firm, Johnson, Rietbrock & Halsey, who had at their disposal 50,000 acres of farm land in Marathon county. In that year Andrew Kreutzer, acting as their agent, took a body of Germans from Grafton, Ozaukee county, to Black Creek Falls (Athens), where they built a mill and began a settlement. Kreutzer frequently visited New York to meet and secure immigrants. The majority of the settlers are the sons of German farmers from the southern part of the State; but with them are people from Brandenburg, Mecklenburg, Limnitz, Pomerania, South Germany, and Austria. They bought hard-wood lands. The census of 1890 indicates an increase of 4,256 — or nearly 100 per cent — of German-born since 1880, of whom the majority probably settled in the western towns, named after the Milwaukee firm, — Halsey, Rietbrock, and Johnson.

West of the Wisconsin River, there are several groups of North Germans. In the vicinity of Wonewoc, including the towns of Summit and Lindina, Juneau county, Hillsborough and Greenwood, Vernon county, Woodland and

Lavalle, Sauk county, there are about 50 Pomeranian families, twelve from Mecklenburg-Schwerin, and single families from several other northern provinces, with a large number of Hanoverians. A few settled there in 1857 and 1867, but the majority came between 1870 and 1875, before a railroad went through—the Chicago & Northwestern railroad having been built through Wonewoc in 1875. Among these immigrants were mechanics, masons, and shoemakers, but the majority were day-laborers, and brought little means — one of the first families (1867) sent $1,100 to Germany, to bring over nine persons. They bought land of speculators, and this proved a disadvantage. There were few accessible markets before the railroad went through, and prices for farm products were low. The settlers were compelled by the land owners to sell their farm products for store-orders, and for several years they were unable to get cash payments. In the town and vicinity of Elroy, joining them on the north, is a group of about 30 Pomeranian families from the districts of Köslin and Stettin, three families from Arnswalde, Brandenburg, and one from Mecklenburg, who settled there about 1880. Of this number only two owned land in Germany, the rest were laborers. Here they worked on the railroad or at any available employment, until they could buy land. Wages they found to be three or four times those obtainable in Germany. In the towns of Honey Creek and Troy, Sauk county, are a number of Pomeranians, and in Greenfield and Fairfield are some Mecklenburgers.

In Buffalo county, the Swiss element prevails, but Canton, one of the northern townships, is settled chiefly with North Germans. They are also found in large numbers among the Swiss in the south-central townships.

In La Crosse county, living in the city of La Crosse and vicinity, are many West Prussians, the majority of whom came between 1875 and 1885.

Besides the North German groups above enumerated, there are scattered settlements in the northwestern part of Wisconsin. Some are from our southern counties, but

many came directly from Germany. Along the line of the
Chicago, St. Paul, Minneapolis & Omaha railway and
through its agency, there are, in Shell Lake, Washburn
county, and Perley and Turtle Lake, Barron county, Germans who came directly from Pomerania and Brandenburg.
At Butternut and Glidden, on the Wisconsin Central railway, there are many West Prussians.

The larger proportion of the North Germans in the
State live upon farms, and came from the agricultural districts of Germany. Predominant among those from the
north-eastern provinces, are day-laborers on the large estates, and small peasant owners. Next come the shepherds,
handicraftsmen, and foresters; a small percentage were
skilled workmen, tradesmen, and large land owners. Of
the earlier immigrants, a large proportion came from Pomerania,[1] especially from the district of Stettin, which is the
most fertile portion, and from Brandenburg and Mecklenburg. In later years, especially since 1876, West Prussia
and Posen have furnished a large portion of the immigrants to Wisconsin. These two provinces, while they
contain large districts of fertile soil, have little enterprise
and a high degree of illiteracy. As a rule, the first emigrants from the various localities were people of some
means, but the great majority brought little money with
them. Often their passage over was prepaid by relatives,
and many went immediately to work in the pineries or
saw-mills, until they were able to secure sufficient means
to purchase land. Often their countrymen here who had
means, or had land to sell, assisted them with loans, not
always to the advantage of the immigrants. The men who
had dealings with these Germans invariably testify that but
small payments were made at first; they nevertheless always
worked and saved enough to make the late payments as
they came due. In almost every community, mention is

---

[1] The estimates indicate that there are now in the State between four
and five thousand German families from Pomerania,— perhaps 25,000 individuals,— by far the largest number from any one province or principality.

made of men who reached here with a few dollars and have since become well-to-do and even wealthy farmers, worth $20,000 or $30,000; while the men who came with considerable property, and after buying farms hired their work done, are now poor men.

In earlier times, the immigrants often brought their primitive plows, axes, and hoes, besides their house-keeping utensils; but they found this unprofitable, and immigrants now rarely bring much besides bedding and clothing. The first generation, especially in the country districts, continue to wear the clothes woven by themselves in the old home. The Pomeranians are occasionally seen with long blue coats brought from Germany; wooden shoes and slippers are used for outdoor work; occasionally, at communion service, men wear the bridegroom's costume of velvet trousers and waistcoat, bought fifty or more years ago. With the second generation, all these peculiarities disappear.

NORTHWESTERN GERMANY.

The population west of the Elbe, including Holstein, is almost entirely of Low Saxon stock who have been there for generations, and among them are some of the purest representatives of the German race.

The Friesians, who dwell along the sea coast in Oldenburg, Hanover, and Western Holstein, still speak a language much like the Dutch, and are distinguished for their strength of character, high-mindedness, and independence. The peasant class here are largely proprietors; political independence has been fostered to some extent, and they are distinguished for their tenacity to old customs.

The people of Schleswig–Holstein are characterized by a somewhat prevalent materialism.[1] Their location on the sea-coast has brought them into contact with other peoples, so that they are less conservative than their countrymen in the interior.

---

[1] Steinhard, ii, p. 736.

The Westphalian peasants, dwelling near the headwaters of the Ems, rival the Frieslanders in their fidelity to old traditions and customs.   These descendants of the old Saxon race are the most conservative element in Germany. Many of their farm-houses are even now built in the same style as in the time of Charlemagne.[1] Here, as in Lippe-Detmold, there is a strong sentiment against the division of the peasant farms.   The Westphalian peasant has but few children, and most of the work is done by laborers.

From Northwestern Germany, there are a few especially interesting groups.   In Manitowoc county, people from Hanover are not distinguished from Mecklenburgers.   In Sheboygan county, a group of several families from Hameln located in the town of Herman about 1847; and a few years later, Hanoverians settled in the towns of Sheboygan and Sheboygan Falls.

In Dane county, in the towns of Windsor and Burke, there is a group of Germans from the village of Strait, in Brunswick.   The first settler came in 1846, a young man of 26; writing of his success, other young men followed him, and later two or three families at a time.   There were, altogether, twenty-two single persons and ten families; some were farmers, the rest weavers, masons, blacksmiths, butchers, and carpenters.   The locality in which they settled was very unlike the one they left, and they had but little means to start with, yet they now own farms of from 40 to 200 acres each, and are regarded among the well-to-do of the neighborhood.   All were originally Lutherans, but about half of them have become Methodists here, and all are rapidly becoming Americanized.

In the vicinity of Wonewoc, Juneau county, there are about 56 families of Hanoverians, who settled there with the Pomeranians in the latter part of the 60's and the 70's. The towns of Westfield and Reedsburg, in Sauk county, are almost entirely settled by people from Hanover.

Oldenburgers settled in large numbers in Liberty and

---

[1] Elisée Reclus, *The Earth and Its Inhabitants*, Europe, iii, p. 280.

Two Rivers, Manitowoc county, and in Calumet county, in the early years of their settlement. They were also among the early settlers in Theresa, Dodge county, in Sheboygan Falls, and later in Shawano county.

Westphalians form few groups in Wisconsin, though many are scattered about the State. In the latter part of the 30's, a group of Westphalians—and with them, people from Cleves—are said to have settled in Kenosha county, but I have not been able to learn more about the settlement. In the early 40's, Westphalians in considerable numbers settled in Newton and Kossuth, Manitowoc county. They, with the people from the Rhine, formed a large portion of the population of the county in 1848.

The early settlers in Neshoto and Mishicott, Manitowoc county, were people from Holstein, who settled there through the influence of Frederick Burchhardt. In Schleswig, Manitowoc county, and New Holstein, Calumet county, there is a group of Germans from Holstein, who came in 1848 and 1849, on account of political discontent. They were mostly men of means, of the agricultural class, but among them were a professor of language, an editor from the city of Altona, a physician, and a poet. The poorer men worked for their wealthier countrymen. They came to Wisconsin through the influence of Ostenfeld, one of their countrymen in Calumet, who visited his native land and called the attention of the people to that portion of Wisconsin. They were men above the average in intelligence, and among them there was an active German life. Theatrical, musical, and debating societies flourished, and there was a decided leaning towards free ideas. The generation now living are more American than German. In addition to these groups, people from Holstein are located in the towns of Fairfield and Greenfield, in Sauk county.

Perhaps the largest group from any one portion of Northwestern Germany is that of "Lippers," from Lippe-Detmold. Lippe-Detmold is a small principality which borders

---

[1] Gustave Körner's *Das Deutsche Element in den Vereinigten Staaten von Nordamerika* (Cincinnati, 1880).

the Weser River on the north, and is intersected by the famous *Teutoberger Wald* at the south. It is mostly mountainous, with rich and fertile valleys; while much of the land is owned by small, independent landowners. The ruling prince possesses large domains which are let out on perpetual lease. It is the custom here for the eldest son to inherit the property, and to make compensation to the other heirs. In this way, the estates are kept undivided for centuries. Spinning flax was the occupation of the people until it was discontinued by reason of the invention of machinery. Overpopulation compelled the inhabitants to migrate during the summer months to Hamburg, Bremen, and Holland to make brick and tile, returning with their earnings in the fall.

Emigration was the result of these economic conditions. The famine year, 1847, was an inciting cause; another was the desire for perfect religious freedom. The Lippers who came to Wisconsin belonged to the Reformed faith. Between 1840 and 1850, a revival occurred in the churches, and the people attended meetings outside of their own districts. This was contrary to official regulations, and though no conflict occurred, the people chafed under legal limitations. Moreover, the old Heidelberg catechism was changed for one of a more rationalistic character. These events probably gave a greater impulse to emigration.

The first emigration from Lippe-Detmold went to St. Louis, whither one of their countrymen, Rev. H. A. Winter,[1] had preceded them. This was in 1847, and the same year another large body came to Wisconsin from near Langenholzhausen, a region bordering on the Weser River, where large domains exist and the villagers are often very poor. About a hundred families, it is thought, came under the leadership of Frederick Reineking and others, and settled in Sheboygan and Manitowoc counties — through the influence of their countryman, Herman Kemper, of Milwaukee, who was an agent for lands in those

---

[1] Now a clergyman in Madison, Wis

counties. They continued to come for the next five or six
years. The majority settled in the western part of Herman, Sheboygan county, in the eastern part of Rhine, in
the neighborhood of Johnsonville, in the town of Sheboygan Falls, and in the city of Sheboygan. In Manitowoc
county they are located in Newton, Centreville, the city of
Manitowoc, and a few in Kossuth and Cooperstown. Their
number is hard to estimate; but with the small groups
situated in various parts of the State, it is thought that
altogether they number over 300 families. The first settlers were poor, and were compelled to work in the saw-
mills. They bought government land, and mortgaged it;
but the debts were soon paid, and success was attained.
One family of eight brothers, who came as poor young
men, are now all well-to-do. In some localities, the Lippers have become Methodists, Baptists, or Presbyterians,
but in Sheboygan county they are still members of the
Reformed church. At Franklin, in the town of Herman,
they have a Reformed college and mission house, founded
on the German mission house plan.

SOUTH AND MIDDLE GERMANY.

The largest groups from South and Middle Germany are
from Rhenish Prussia, Switzerland,[1] Bavaria, Luxemburg,
Baden, and Saxony. There are also many Hessians, Wür-
temburgers, and Germans from Austria.

The South and Middle Germans were among the earlier
settlers, especially those of 1848 to 1854. They are found
in largest numbers in our eastern counties. In Milwaukee,
they form the larger proportion of the German population; this is true, also, of Fond du Lac, Oshkosh, and
Menasha. They are found also in large numbers in Washington, Milwaukee, Ozaukee, Jefferson, Dane, Sauk, and
Buffalo counties. Besides these early settlements, another

---

[1] Not politically a part of Germany, but the population is chiefly
German, and the historical conditions are similar to those of Germany.

large group was formed in the 80's, in north-central Wisconsin.

The majority of the South Germans are Catholics.[1] The large German Catholic immigration to the State is probably due in some measure to the fact that a German priest and bishop were early sent to Milwaukee, both of them well-known and of marked ability.   In 1844, Bishop Henni, a native of Switzerland, was sent to Milwaukee from Cincinnati, where he had been professor of philosophy and church history in the Athenaeum.   He had founded many German Catholic societies in Ohio and had established the first German Catholic newspaper in America.   He was a man of strong German spirit, and through his instrumentality a *priester seminar* was established, which afterwards became the nucleus of a large group of institutions at St. Francis.   When he went to Milwaukee in 1844, there were, according to Schem,[2] but eight thousand Catholics in Wisconsin; but in 1867 there were two hundred and fifty thousand, the increase being largely due to Bishop Henni's direction and increasing activity.   Thus the Milwaukee diocese became one of the most important in the United States, and Henni was made archbishop, being the first German in the United States to attain that office.[3]   He has been followed by German bishops, not only in Milwaukee, but also in Green Bay and La Crosse.

RHENISH PRUSSIA.

From the earliest years, the Rhine River has been one of the chief waterways of Europe.   It was the highway of immigration, and many a fierce struggle was fought on its banks.   It has always been characterized by a vigorous

---

[1] Some idea of the proportion of North and South Germans in Wisconsin, can be obtained from the statistics of the German Lutheran and German Catholic churches.   There were in 1893, according to church authorities, about 225,000 German Lutherans and 105,000 German Catholics in Wisconsin.

[2] Schem, *Deutsch-Amerik, Conversations-Lexicon*, v, p. 266.

[3] Körner, p. 290.

and varied life. Owing to the rich mines of ore that lie embedded in the mountains bordering the Rhine, and on account of its fertile meadows, industry is probably more varied than elsewhere in Germany. Vine-culture, coal, iron mining, manufacturing, and agriculture, are the chief industries.[1]

The vineyards lie mainly between Mayence and Bonn, including the district of Cologne, and along the valleys of the Mosel and Neckar. In the vine regions, the scenery is picturesque. In the Rhine valley, the inhabitants are a fiery, nervous race, having a strong attachment to their homes, and hospitable and socially inclined. The country is rich in poetry and song, and the German good cheer (*gemüthlichkeit*) reigns supreme. The Mosel valley is a relatively isolated region; owing to the former lack of communication with the outside world, the history and legends bear much more of a provincial character than those of the Rhine, while its inhabitants are less progressive.[2]

Of the industrial regions, the towns of Elberfeld and Barmen, in the Wupper valley, are the most famous for the variety and excellence of their manufactures, which can hardly be excelled in all Germany. Physically, the men, owing to the kind of labor they perform, are less developed than in the mountainous regions.

The population of the Rhinelands is more than one-half Roman Catholic. The Protestant element, which, by the census of 1880, numbers over a million, is strongest on the right bank of the river. In the valley of the Wupper, the Reformed faith prevails. Rhineland is one of the most thickly-populated regions of Germany.

The Rhenish Prussians located in Wisconsin are chiefly from the government districts of Cologne (Köln) and Treves, which includes the Mosel valley, and from Elberfeld and Barmen, in the Wupper valley. They were among the earliest German immigrants to the State, and include small

[1] *Grossindustrie, Rheinlands und Westfalen.*
[2] Steinhard, ii, pp. 308–315.

24

peasant farmers from the vine regions, and many of the industrial class. In 1841 and 1842 a few individuals located in different places, and opened the way for the larger settlements. In 1841, it is said that a few families from near Cologne settled at Oak Creek, Milwaukee county. In 1842 Christian Peil, from the same locality, settled in the town of Lake. He wrote home to his friends, and soon after six families followed, among them the Deusters; within a few years, fifty or more families (all Catholics) emigrated and settled either in the town of Lake, where the settlement was named New Köln, or in Oak Creek. Some were men of considerable means, and none were compelled to leave their native land because of poverty. Rhenish Prussians settled also at West Granville; but whether they came with the Köln settlers, I have not learned. Of the earlier settlers and their families, but few remain. These towns are almost solidly German, but their population is a mixed one, composed of representatives of all portions of the "Fatherland."

About the same time, people from the Rhine settled in Dane, Sauk, Fond du Lac, Manitowoc, Sheboygan, and Outagamie counties, locating usually near Catholic mission stations. Count Haraszthy opened the way to German settlement along the Wisconsin at Sauk City, and on the opposite bank, as early as 1840.[1] In Dane county, a mission station was formed in 1845 at Roxbury, presided over by a German Catholic priest. Large German settlements were soon formed, the majority of the settlers being Rhenish Prussians. The Wisconsin River, at Sauk City, was thought to resemble a portion of the Rhenish territory, and this was another reason for the German settlement there. A large number from all parts of this province are settled in the town of Prairie du Sac. At Roxbury, Cross Plains, Middleton, and Berry, in Dane county, the Germans are from Cologne and other portions of Rhenish Prussia, and from Bavaria. In Madison, a German Catholic priest was

---

[1] See sketch of Haraszthy, *ante*, pp. 79, 80.—ED.

located in 1849. The congregation was chiefly Irish, few Germans being then settled there; but in that year Gov. L. J. Farwell bought the Doty claim, and began to improve the lands between the two lakes and the Catfish River. His object was to dig a canal connecting the lakes, and to build a mill. Through immigration agents, he invited Germans to come in, and many arrived that year from different parts of the old country. During the next decade, there was so large an increase, that the parish was divided into Irish and German congregations in 1853.[1]

In Fond du Lac county, the first families from Rhenish Prussia located about 1841 in the town of Calumet, which then included Marshfield. This was along the east shore of Lake Winnebago, which they reached from Sheboygan. The first settlers attracted others, and by 1845 a Catholic church was built at Marytown. It was the only one for miles around, and became a strong center of attraction. Owing to the bad harvest of 1846, in Germany, the immigration was especially large that year; while the agitations of 1848 and 1849, with the increased demand for military service, drove away many others.

Dr. Carl de Haas, in a work written in 1848,[2] stated that the inhabitants of the Calumet settlement then numbered 1,500, of whom only about twenty German families were Protestants; the rest were Catholics, mostly from the Rhine territory, many from Mosel, already forming by far the greater part of the population, and increasing daily. By 1850, the towns of Calumet, Marshfield, Taycheedah, and Forest were settled by Germans who were mostly Rhinelanders from the districts of Cologne and Treves.

Between 1850 and 1856, people from the same district in Germany settled in Ashford, in the southeastern part of the county; and at about the same time, in the city of

---

[1] The original German congregation in Madison contained nineteen Bavarian families, seven from Würtemberg, six from Baden, nine from Switzerland, and nine from the Rhine provinces.

[2] *Nord Amerika Wisconsin, Calumet: Winke für Auswanderer* (Elberfeld and Iserlohn, 1848).

Fond du Lac. Outside of the city, belonging to five Catholic churches in these towns, there are over 560 families,
mainly from the Rhine provinces. They live in the above-
mentioned towns, and in less numbers in Eden, Osceola,
and Lamartine. In Germany, they were farmers on their
own estates, and mechanics. Nearly all brought means
enough to enable them to buy either government land or
improved farms. They now each own from 40 to 160 acres
of land, and all are comfortably circumstanced, though
they are said not to exhibit as much pride in the mainte-
nance of their buildings as the North Germans, in Dodge
county.

In Outagamie county, there is a large group living in
the city of Appleton and in the towns of Freedom, Center,
Ellington, Dale, and Greenville. It is thought that the first
Germans settled in Buchanan as early as 1842. A Catholic
mission was formed at Little Chute, presided over by
Father T. J. Van den Broek,[1] and here again the church
was a special attraction. They came from all parts of
Rhenish Prussia, and were nearly all possessed of means —
all the way from $200 to $1,200. The majority settled
there in the 50's, and bought either government land, or
that owned by the Green Bay & Mississippi Canal Co.
Some Germans were employed in the construction of that
canal. Here, many of them own farms of 160 acres, and
are a well-to-do people.

In Manitowoc and Sheboygan counties, the Rhenish
Prussians were among the earlier settlers. About 1846 and
1847, some five families located in Newton. The next body
was induced to settle through Charles Esslinger, later a
citizen of Manitowoc. For several years he was located in
Buffalo as agent of the firm of Jones & Allen, who
owned considerable land about Manitowoc. During the
winter of 1849-50, a body of Rhinelanders — 56 persons in
all, he tells me — were compelled to remain in Buffalo.

---

[1] See *ante*, "Documents relating to the Catholic church in Green Bay,"
pp. 192 *et seq.*— ED.

Esslinger met them and persuaded them to locate in Manitowoc county. Some remained in the town, but most
of them settled on farms in Newton, while a few located in
Kossuth. Newton now contains a large Rhenish Prussian
element, particularly from Elberfeld and Barmen; but some
also are from Wesel, probably induced to settle through
the influence of Gustav Richter, who was a native of that
place.[1]

In Sheboygan county, the Rhinelanders are settled in the
town of Rhine, having located there about 1847.

Many Rhenish Prussians from the valley of the Wupper,
a tributary of the Rhine, seem to have settled in Wisconsin
about this time. A work written by Theodore Wettstein of
Barmen,[2] who came to the United States as leader of a
large party of settlers, and himself settled in Milwaukee,
states the conditions there, and causes of emigration, and
describes their journey. For a long time, he writes,
streams of emigrants have been leaving Germany; but no
trace of the agitation has reached the Wupper valley,
though affairs are in a bad condition. Manufacturing was
the principal industry there, but it was losing ground owing
to increased competition, which lowered wages and the price
of wares. The laborers and trading classes, he said, suffered most. Emigration was agitated; but with some the
question was, whether they were morally and physically
suited to the hard struggle in the forests of America; with
others, it was a question of means. The reports from the
United States were generally looked upon with suspicion;
but the work written by Dr. de Haas, from Calumet, who
was a native of Elberfeld, was regarded as trustworthy
and widely circulated. By the fall of 1847, about 800 persons in Elberfeld and Barmen had planned to emigrate.
They were mostly handicraftsmen and traders — men of
some means, who expected to enter farms in the West.
Wettstein was one of those who had decided to leave. He

---

[1] See his *Der Nordamerikanische Freistaat Wisconsin* (Wesel, 1849).
[2] *Der Nordamerikanische Freistaat Wisconsin* (Elberfeld, 1851).

had several young sons whose future caused him much anxiety; he felt that the prospects for success were far better in the new world than in Germany. Being a man of some prominence in that locality, having held some important civil positions, many desired to go under his leadership. He gathered a company of 156 persons,— 69 from Barmen, 31 from Elberfeld, and 56 from other cities,— and engaged passage at $40 a head. He seems to have started with a preference for Wisconsin, and in New York his impressions were confirmed. He came to Milwaukee, and though no definite statement is made regarding the matter, he implies that the majority accompanied him. Just where they settled I have not learned, but very likely in Milwaukee, Manitowoc, and Sheboygan counties, for about that time people from Wettstein's district located in those counties.

In Menasha, the largest element in the German Catholic church is from the valley of the Mosel.

LUXEMBURG.

The grand duchy of Luxemburg is a small triangular state, situated on the eastern slope of the Ardennes mountains, and separated from Rhenish Prussia by the Mosel River. The northern triangle, which, like the province of Luxemburg, consists of broad tracts of table-land, with an unfruitful soil and sparse population, is known as the Oesling; the southern portion bears the name of Gutland. The latter, as its name indicates, is a more fruitful region, with rich fields, well-watered meadows, and a denser population. The Mosel drains the country; and along its banks, as in Rhenish Prussia, the vine grows in abundance.

Like Belgium, Luxemburg has constantly been exposed to the rapacity of stronger nations; the character and disposition of her people bear many traces of foreign influence. After a few centuries of self rule, following the breaking up of the Kingdom of the Franks, Luxemburg became a fief of Burgundy in 1447. Then in 1506, it passed in succession to the Spanish branch of the house of Hapsburg; to the Austrian branch of the same house in 1714, and at length, in 1796, was taken possession of by the French republic. In 1815 it was united with Holland and Belgium into the Kingdom of the Netherlands. In 1830 this arrangement was broken up by the revolt of Belgium and a portion of Luxemburg, and in 1839 Luxemburg was divided between Holland and Belgium — the grand duchy which contains the larger portion of the country being united with Holland by a personal union. Finally, in 1867, after a long diplomatic controversy between France and Germany, the neutrality of the grand duchy was declared. Thus Luxemburg can hardly be said to have had any national life. It neither shared the French nor the German regeneration of national feeling in this century. The result of this is a degree of cosmopolitanism not generally found in Germany, and a hatred of military service, which had never been called out in behalf of their own country, but for a foreign ruling power. In spite, however, of this variety of foreign influences, the Luxemburgers have remained a comparatively distinct people, possessing their own characteristics and customs, and have remained true to the Roman Catholic church.

Luxemburgers are mostly of German descent. They are of Frankish, mixed with the Saxon stock which was introduced into this region by Charlemagne; but they also contain some French elements, brought in to re-people the country after the devastation of the Thirty Years' War.[1] The dialect is middle high German — strong and irregular, by reason of the peculiar pronunciation of the diphthongs, as well as by a coloring of neighboring idioms, especially the French.[2]

In its political history, Luxemburg has shared the experience of Europe in this century. Until the French republic proclaimed the sovereignty of the people and the destruction of feudalism, Luxemburg had retained the

[1] Schottes's *Geschichte des Luxemburger Landes*, i, p. 304.
[2] Groewigs's, *Luxemburg*, p. 6.

feudal conditions of the middle ages. The reforms of
Maria Theresa were not introduced into the Netherlands,
and the old privileges of the orders and cities were not in-
terfered with.[1] During the union with Holland (1815–30),
Luxemburg had much to suffer from the attempt to unite
opposing elements represented in differences of public
spirit, religion, language, and industries. An attempt was
made to introduce the Dutch as the national language.
New taxes were laid, which fell heaviest on the agricultural classes; it was these taxes, with a duty on wine, that
caused the emigration to Brazil, and started the Luxemburgers across the sea.[2] In spite of these wrongs, Luxemburg owes to the union with Holland the restoration of
local government and the building up of education, both of
which had suffered from French influences.[3] The demo-
cratic constitution adopted by Belgium, in which freedom
of the press and direct elections were established, and
equality proclaimed, had a profound effect upon Luxemburg, so that when a restricted constitution was granted
to the grand duchy in 1840, complaints grew so loud that
it was revised in 1848 [4]

Though the emigration from Luxemburg was largely the
result of economic conditions, which especially affected
the agricultural classes, yet the discontent that followed
the restoration in 1839, and the restricted constitution,
doubtless added to the emigrating impulse. Another cause
was the dislike of military service, which, as above stated,
is the result of foreign rule, and the unwillingness of the
people to expose their lives for a foreign nation. For that
reason many young men withdrew from the Holland, and

---

[1] Wolf's *Austria* (Oncken Series), p. 118.

[2] Nicholas Gonner's *Die Luxemburger in der Neuen Welt* (Dubuque,
Iowa, 1889). This is a valuable work, from which I have obtained many
of my facts relating to the Wisconsin immigration of Luxemburgers.

[3] Marquardsen's *Handbuch des Oeffentlichen Rechts*, Luxemburg, iv:
i. 4, ii Halfte, 11–15.

[4] *Ibid.*, p. 18. In the revision, censorship of the press was removed, and
the suffrage greatly enlarged.

later from the Belgian, service during the wars that occurred between 1830 and 1839.

The heaviest emigration[1] from Luxemburg began in the
40's.   In 1842, New York and Ohio received the most of
these immigrants, but in 1845 large numbers came to Illinois and Wisconsin.   The first arrivals in Wisconsin settled in Port Washington.   Following them came a body of
fifteen families who settled at Holy Cross, in Fredonia,
Ozaukee county.   One of the company had previously re-
sided in Ohio.   They were from the cantons of Redingen and
Capellen, and from the province of Luxemburg, on the
Belgian frontier.[2]   John Longeley opened a hotel at Port.
Washington, and soon after some of his countrymen followed him and bought up land, which they afterwards dis-
posed of to later immigrants.   The year 1846 brought many
more.   Some eight or ten families bought land in the vicinity of the Lake Church (St. Mary am See), in the town
of Port Washington; in the same year, many from the province of Luxemburg settled in the town of Belgium, and
gave it its name.   In 1847, people from the Mosel settled
in Port Washington, and with them were several from
Rhineland, the Eifel, Hunsrück,[3] and from the Gâ, or
region between the Sauer and Mosel.   Others settled near
St. Nicholas, or Dacada, just over the line in Sheboygan
county, where by 1848 there were nearly eighty Luxemburg families.   In 1848, about eight families from Mach-
thurn and Niederdonven, on the Mosel, in the canton of
Grevenmacher, settled in Pewaukee, Waukesha county.

Thus between 1845 and 1848, perhaps a hundred and fifty
or more families, chiefly from the Belgian frontier and
the region of the Mosel, had settled in Wisconsin.   The

---

[1] They came from the villages of Türpen, Selingen, Flaxheim, Battin-
court, Herzog, Kleinelter, Guirsh, Kientzig, Offen, and Sterpenich.

[2] Gonner, pp. 96, 216.

[3] The Eifel and Hunsrück much resemble the Oesling of Luxemburg.
The inhabitants obtain only a scant existence by agriculture, stock raising,
and mining, while many go to Holland each spring to obtain work.

.settlement here was due to the favorable reports which
had been circulated.   A letter quoted by Gonner from the
Luxemburger Wort,' says: "The State of Wisconsin is the
region which the Luxemburgers prefer for settlement.
The soil is productive, the climate similar to that in the
grand duchy, the necessaries of life are cheap, and employment can be obtained."   Another inducement for the
settlement was, that the Luxemburger almost universally
preferred the forest.² In New York, Ohio, and Wisconsin
they chose woodland.   The reason for this preference,
aside from the desire to obtain fuel and building material,
is the fact that the forests have become scarce in their
native land, and a piece of woodland is regarded as a
treasure; it marks the difference between the small and
large peasant estates.

Owing to the failure of harvests in 1854, emigration was
especially large from 1854 to 1857.   It is estimated that
6,000 persons left Luxemburg at that time.   A few only,
remained in New York and Ohio; a large number settled
near Milwaukee and along Lake Michigan; some joined the
original settlers in Pewaukee, and small groups located at
Luxemburg, Kewaunee county, St. Joseph's Ridge, in La
Crosse county, and in the mineral region near Potosi, in
southwestern Wisconsin.   During the next three decades,
emigration from Luxemburg continued, and Wisconsin received a considerable part of it.

At present, Luxemburgers, both from the duchy and the
Belgian province, are found scattered throughout the State.
The largest settlement is in the neighborhood of Port
Washington.   It extends northward for several miles into
Sheboygan county, west from Lake Michigan, into the
towns of Fredonia and Saukville, Washington county; and
for several miles south of Port Washington.   There are
about 500 Luxemburg families in this latter locality, belonging to the four Catholic congregations of Port Wash-

¹ II jahrgang 1849, March 16 (Gonner, p. 97).
² Gonner, pp. 108, 109, 162.

ington, Holy Cross, St. Mary am See, and St. Nicholas church near Dacada.[1]

The early settlers in the town of Belgium were young men with little means, and nearly all of the peasant class. Port Washington has an excellent harbor, and in the early days a busy trade was carried on there. Ozaukee county was a dense, hard-wood forest, but the soil was good, and it was soon cleared. The immigrants had brought with them some tools from home, such as axes, plows, hoes, even wagons,—but they were unsuited to our soil. At first, times were hard and wages low. The settlers sold cord-wood at the piers along the lake shore. Wheat, at first their only product, brought forty or fifty cents a bushel.

The Luxemburg farms in Wisconsin are not large, owing partly to the prevalence of the old Luxemburg custom of dividing the land among the several sons; yet they are a prosperous and well-to-do people. Few American farmers now remain in that vicinity.

BAVARIA.

The kingdom of Bavaria, lying between the Alps and the Fichtel and Bohemian mountains, is an extensive plateau drained by the Danube and Maine rivers, with their tributaries. About a fourth of the country is covered with forests, which are chiefly found in Upper and Lower Bavaria, and the Upper Palatinate. In the south, the land is largely used for pasturage and cattle. Most of the land owners are peasant proprietors, living in villages. Many manufactures are carried on, among them extensive glass works in the Böhmerwald. The kingdom also includes the Bavarian Palatinate, which lies on the left bank of the Rhine.

---

[1] Of the other groups, there are about seventy-five families located in Milwaukee, Granville, and St. Francis; perhaps thirty families in the northeastern part of Washington county; between fifty and sixty families at Theresa and Lomira; and nearly fifty families in Outagamie county, near Appleton and Kaukauna.

The inhabitants are Old Bavarians who dwell in the eastern part, in Upper and Lower Bavaria, and in the Upper Palatinate; Franks, dwelling in the west; Swabians, in Swabia and Neuberg; and Rhinelanders, on the Rhine. The Old Bavarians are a strong, simple, credulous race; they show great deference to authority, both political and ecclesiastical; until recent years, the Bavarian schools have been neglected, and education there is below the average. The Swabians are large of body, and are both more easily moved and more apt to learn than the Bavarians. The Rhenish Bavarians excel the Swabians in bodily size and versatility, and distinguish themselves by the spirit of undertaking. The Lutheran is the state church of Bavaria, but the Catholic population is very large.

The largest Bavarian groups in Wisconsin are from the vicinity of the village of Wunsiedel, near Baireuth, in the Fichtel mountains, where small farms exist; from the Bohemian mountains near Eger and Zwiesel, and from the forests of Lower Bavaria; there are also many from Rhenish Bavaria and other parts of the country. They are located in Jefferson, Dane, Sauk, and Manitowoc counties; in the cities of Fond du Lac, Oshkosh, and Appleton, and along the Wisconsin Central railway, north of Stevens Point.

In Dane county, the Bavarians are located in the towns of Roxbury, Cross Plains, and the city of Madison, these settlements being formed in the 40's.

About the same time, a Bavarian settlement was made at Columbus, early known as New Franken.

In Jefferson county, there is a large group located in the city and town of Jefferson, and in the towns of Aztalan, Farmington, and Hebron. They are from the vicinity of Wunsiedel, in the province of Oberfranken, and first came to Wisconsin in 1847, continuing the immigration until 1860. A Lutheran church was organized in 1851, with 64 members; in 1857 the same congregation numbered 108 families, of whom a part were North Germans. There are now about a hundred Bavarian Lutheran families in that vicinity, and many more who are Catholics. In Germany, these people were peasants and mechanics; here, they are mostly farmers, living on their own land. Between 1845 and 1854, about fifteen families from the Rhenish Palatinate located in Watertown and vicinity; about eight families still remain, who are connected with the Catholic church.

In Menasha, a German Catholic congregation of about 250 families contains a large Bavarian element. They arrived in Menasha about 1858. Many of them are still there, working in the paper mills and factories; others have settled on farms in the vicinity of Neenah.

In Appleton and vicinity, besides the large number of Rhenish Prussians, there are many Bavarians and German Bohemians, from the vicinity of Zwiesel, Carlsbad, Eger, and Folkenow, on the border line between Bavaria and Bohemia. As many as fifty families are located in the third and fourth wards of Appleton; another group from the same locality, is to be found in the Sugar Bush settlement, near Seymour; still others are to be found in Buchanan. The Bavarian forest land near Zwiesel is poor soil, and many of the immigrants to Outagamie county had been employed in the glass factories and grist mills of that part of Bavaria; they rarely brought means with them. German Bohemians from the same locality have also settled in Greenville, Ellington, and Center, in the same county.

In the Catholic churches of Oshkosh, there are between 400 and 500 Bavarians and German Bohemians. A few Bavarians are also found in the Lutheran churches.

In Leroy, Dodge county, a Bavarian settlement was formed about 1861, consisting of perhaps eleven or twelve families from the Upper Palatinate and Lower Bavaria.

A more recent immigration from Bavaria, is that into north-central Wisconsin, which occurred between 1879 and 1889. This movement was due largely to the efforts of Kent K. Kennan and Johann B. Ferstl. According to Mr. Kennan's statement, Zwiesel was the center of the Wisconsin emigration which he induced. The people came from the Bavarian forests, northwest of Munich.[1] They were peasants, woodcutters, mill-laborers, and handicrafts-men of various sorts— said to be strong, hardy folk, better adapted than the Swiss to life in the forests, and espe-cially better for that life than the so-called *fabrikarbeiter* from the cities. It is roughly estimated that about 5,000 Germans settled in the State, especially along the Wiscon-sin Central railway, in Clark, Taylor, Price, and Ashland counties, and that nine-tenths were from Bavaria.

The causes of this Bavarian emigration, according to Ferstl, were three: (1) The low wages for laborers, es-pecially in the forest regions of *Nieder Bayern;* (2) the un-productiveness (*Unrentabilität*) of agriculture; (3) the con-stant dread of war.[2] The low rates of travel at that time, were also a special inducement.[3] Nearly all paid their own fare to Wisconsin; the majority brought means enough to buy land, while the rest were obliged to earn their farms. Nearly all were particular to settle near their own people; they came in groups of several families from the same lo-cality. Once or twice a year, Kennan personally conducted parties of emigrants to the State.[4] While the Bavarian element doubtless predominates among these people, there are also many Austrians and Swiss, and representatives of all parts of Germany.[5]

---

[1] Letters were written for *Der Ansiedler*, of Milwaukee, by men from vil-lages near Teplitz, Bohemia; Schattau, Mähren, Austria, and Heidenreich-stein, Lower Austria; and from Unter-Franken, Bavaria.

[2] Most of those who came to Wisconsin had performed military service.

[3] A notice in *Der Ansiedler* of June 15, 1881, announces that tickets from Antwerp to Milwaukee, were for sale at their office for $39.

[4] For example, in the fall of 1881 a body of 150 persons accompanied him, and were soon followed by 75 others. Some went to Black Creek Falls and Butternut, but the majority remained in the immigrant house at Medford, waiting to buy land in that locality, or to find employment.

[5] So far, I have been unable, except to a limited extent, to locate the miscellaneous German groups. Many settled in the western part of Mara-thon county, with those already mentioned. In 1881 and 1882, a saw-mill was built by a Medford firm, at Bruckerville, a small town four miles east of Dorchester; about it, as in all those northern towns, a black-

The majority of them are Catholics — altogether there are over 1,100 Catholic families, or between 5,000 and 6,000 people; of these, 572 families settled in Wood county, chiefly at Marshfield, and 185 in Clark county. There are also nine Lutheran societies, which are comparatively small — Black Creek Falls (about 40 families), Dorchester, Colby, Stetsonville, Medford, Whittlesey, Chelsea, town of Brannon, Phillips, Butternut (85 families), Glidden (25 families), Ashland, Shell Lake, and Deer Park.

BADEN.

Baden includes three districts, — the Black Forest, Odenwald, and the eastern valley of the Rhine. It contains a greater proportion of forest land than any other part of Germany, and eighty per cent of the territory is mountainous. While the inhabitants of the forest are less versatile and enlightened than those of the Rhine valley, they are more powerful, moral, and contented — but, except in the Odenwald, not so well-to-do. The Lutheran is the state

---

smith shop, some stores, and a few houses collected, and it became a post-office and market. A letter from a German farmer in that region, dated October, 1882, mentions six families from the neighborhood of Teplitz, Bohemia, who had settled between Dorchester and Poniatowski. At Bruckerville, there were also several Saxon families. A Bavarian from Unter-Franken writes in *Der Ansiedler* for April 1, 1881, from Poniatowski, that many relatives and friends have settled with him. Letters to the same paper, of February 1, 1882, mention three families from Schattau, Mähren, Austria, and one from Heidenreichstein, Lower Austria, settled at Black Creek Falls and Dorchester. According to a letter to *Der Ansiedler* for February 15, 1883, there is at Little Black River, south of Medford, a German settlement composed of people from Westphalia, Saxony, Würtemburg, and Austria. Many German settlers in northern Wisconsin are from the southern part of this State. In both Butternut, Ashland county, and Black Creek Falls, Marathon county, there are about 20 families from near Milwaukee. At Whittlesey, Taylor county, there are some six families from Sheboygan. At Butternut and Glidden, besides the West Prussians mentioned above, there are some Saxons, and from eight to sixteen families of Bavarians in each. In Fifield, there are some German Bohemians.

church, but the Roman Catholics greatly outnumber the Protestants, and are strongest in the south.

Emigration from Baden received a great impulse from the Revolution of 1848. Baden was one of the first countries to be affected by the French Revolution, not only because of its proximity to that country, but from the "tendencies of the lively and susceptible race that inhabit it."[1]

Some of this emigration came to Wisconsin — there being two important groups, so far as I can ascertain, in Marion, Grant county, and Eaton, Manitowoc county. The former settlement was made in 1854 by stone-cutters and masons from Heidelberg and Freiburg. In 1847, several men with their families, hoping for better economic conditions in the new world, left Heidelberg with scarcely more than enough means to carry them across the ocean. They settled in Ulster, New York, where they found work in the quarries. In 1849, a second body of men who had been engaged in the revolutionary uprisings, stole out of Germany into France, and with their families sailed to America and joined the first group in Ulster. Among these were men of some means, who brought with them several hundred dollars apiece. In 1851, a third body of men from Heidelberg, hearing good reports from the earlier emigrants, came to Lancaster, Grant county, Wisconsin. The New York settlers worked there until 1854, but fearing that the quarries would be exhausted, and desirous of owning land, began to search for a suitable locality. Having heard of the good lands, water, and timber of Wisconsin, they sent two of their number, Christopher Brechler and Joseph Heim, to visit the State and report. They came to Mineral Point, where one of the land offices was located, and thence went out to Marion, where they found wood, water, and climate much like that in their German homes. They did not wish prairie land, and this locality was much to their taste. The committee bought enough government land for all their friends. Returning to New York, their report was satis-

---

[1] Sybel's *Founding of the German Empire*, i, p. 147.

factory, and in the fall of 1854 all of the New York settlers sold out and came to Wisconsin. The same year, the emigrants of 1851 to Lancaster, joined the other party in Marion. Since 1854, this settlement has drawn steadily from different parts of Germany, and now numbers between 200 and 225 individuals. They have bought all the farms that have been offered for sale, gradually taking possession of land once owned by Americans. Their farms, it is reported, range from 80 to 600 acres, the average being perhaps 300 acres. Their houses, fences, and stock are all good, and they have particularly fine horses. New land is constantly broken, and everything is done with characteristic thoroughness. This is a distinctively German community; its members intermarry with Germans, maintain their own schools, and teach their children to speak German. The people belong to two congregations,— a German Presbyterian and a Lutheran; the former maintain a church and minister in their own locality, while the Lutherans attend the church at Boscobel.

In the same year (1854), a Baden community of a very different character was formed in Wisconsin — the St. Nazianz colony, in the town of Eaton, Manitowoc county. Not long after the revolution of 1848, when a spirit of restlessness pervaded Baden, and economic conditions were unusually oppressive, a large body of German Catholics from different parts of the country,— the Black Forest, Klettgau, Breisgau, Schwabia, and Odenwald,— assembled under the leadership of Rev. Ambros Oschwald, a Catholic priest from the district of Freiburg, and emigrated to America. This movement was due to overpopulation, and, as they claimed, to the vexations suffered under Protestant rule — but more especially to the desire to form in America a free Roman Catholic community after their own ideas. It was their common sympathy with the peculiar doctrines taught by their leader, that brought them together. He held the idea of the early apostles as to community of goods, and preached as Paul did concerning marriage,— urging a single life for those not already

25

married. His book, written in support of these ideas, was
condemned by the Catholic authorities, but he found a
body of sympathizers who followed him to America. They
numbered 114 persons, among whom were several families.

Before starting for their new home, they formed a vol-
untary association[1] called the "Colony of St. Nazianz,"
named after a Greek saint, and adopted regulations for
their government. They agreed to be ruled by an "epho-
rate," or senate, of twelve members (the manner of ap-
pointment is not stated) and the presiding priest, who
should act as directors of their public affairs, settling dis-
putes, and watching over the morality of the members.
Their plan was to live as much as possible in common, and
land was to be held as common property. In the spring
of 1854 they left Germany, having as their destination
Milwaukee, where Oschwald had a letter to Bishop Henni
from the archbishop of Freiburg. German Catholics, their
chronicle[2] states, were then flocking to the Western states,
and the immigration to Wisconsin received a great impulse
after the arrival of Henni in Milwaukee. Reaching Milwaukee in August, a house was purchased by their leader
for $900; this was intended to shelter the party until the
way was opened for their settlement. Soon negotiations
for land were entered into, and Oschwald purchased 3,840
acres from Milwaukee agents at $3.50 an acre, paying $1,500
down. Six men were then sent out with the land-dealers
to find the site. They went by boat to Manitowoc, and
thence across the country, at that time a dense wilderness.
There the rest of the colony joined them, and by dint of
hard work the soil was at last brought under cultivation.

In their new home they proceeded to carry out their
ideas. The single men and women were to live in separate
houses or cloisters; two such were built of beams and
plaster, as was the custom in Germany. It was their plan

The articles to which the members gave their assent, were probably
drawn up by their leader, and submitted to them for approval.

[2] A pamphlet account of the affairs of the community, covering the years
1854-1866.

to make themselves independent of the outside world; accordingly, they raised all their own food products and manufactured their own clothing. Peace reigned in the community until the death of their leader, when some difficulties arose concerning the property. It had been held by Oschwald in his own name, and at his death he willed it to the community; but the will was found to be invalid in court, since the society had never been incorporated and was thus incapable of inheriting property. To obviate this difficulty, they proceeded to incorporate the community as the "Roman Catholic Religious Society;" then each member sued the estate for his past services; judgment was allowed and papers were made out, assigning the property to the society.

They are now governed by a board of trustees elected annually by the adult members, both men and women. This board consists of three men and three women, and the presiding priest *ex officio*. They are neither favored nor condemned by the church authorities here. They still wear the German peasant dress, live as they did in the "Fatherland," and in all respects are a simple, primitive, and extremely religious people. Three religious services are held each day. At present they number about 200 adults. To recruit their numbers, orphan children are adopted into the community; but there are few of these, and the society does not seem destined to a long life.

SWISS SETTLEMENTS.

The Swiss in Wisconsin, according to the census of 1890, number 7,181. There are several large groups in the State, from various cantons, located chiefly in Green, Buffalo, Sauk, Fond du Lac, and Taylor counties.

One of the most interesting German settlements in Wisconsin is that of the Swiss in New Glarus, Green county.[1]

---

[1] The history of this settlement is interestingly and carefully told by John Luchsinger, in *Wis. Hist. Colls.*, xii. It is from this source that I have taken the facts related here.

It is notable because of the manner in which the immigration was conducted. Its cause was the business depression that began in Germany about 1844, and "overpopulation in an unfertile country." Land had been divided and subdivided, as population increased. In the canton of Glarus, from which this colony came, the land is allotted in small portions to each citizen for cultivation, and when one emigrates he receives the value of his allotment, as well as the value of his interest in the rest of the common property. This virtually puts a premium on emigration. When the distress had become unendurable, it was decided to attempt organized emigration. A public meeting was held at Schwanden, at which it was decided to ask the co-operation of the government of the canton. This was successful, and fifteen hundred florins were appropriated for the purpose of sending two men to select a suitable tract of land for a colony. An emigration society was formed, and Nicholas Duerst and Fridolin Streiff were selected to choose the land. They were to find a locality similar in climate, soil, and general characteristics to their home in Switzerland, also suitable for raising stock and vegetables, and enough of it so that each colonist who contributed sixty florins might have twenty acres of land.

In March, 1845, they came to America. After searching in vain through Ohio, Indiana, and Illinois, they at length, in August, 1845, found a tract in Green county, Wisconsin, which answered their purpose; it was within thirty-five miles of Mineral Point, then a good market. They bought twelve hundred acres of farm land, and eighty acres of timber.

Meanwhile, the people at home were restless; and to avoid the breaking up of the society it was decided to migrate in April, 1845, instead of waiting until the following year. One hundred and ninety-three persons collected for this emigration, although only 140 had been expected and provided for. Before starting they chose George Legler and Jacob Grob as leaders. After a long journey, with many hard experiences, they reached Baltimore the last of June. From there they went to St. Louis, where they were to await reports from Duerst and Streiff. They rented two houses for temporary shelter, and hearing nothing from their delegates sent two men in search of them. At length, in the middle of August, the colonists reached their destination in Wisconsin. They then numbered only 108, the rest having left from discouragement or to obtain work. Before winter, sixteen log huts were erected. Many had brought furniture and tools, which proved very useful at a time when they were unable to purchase. To tide them over the first year, a thousand dollars was sent them from Switzerland. The land for cultivation was divided among the colonists by lot; but the timber land was held in common. Stock was purchased of drovers from Ohio. The first few years proved difficult, partly on account of their ignorance of American methods of farming. In Switzerland, the land was not adapted to raising grain, and the use of horses and plows was impossible; but with the assistance of American farmers in the vicinity, the emigrants learned to cultivate the land. They early betook themselves to dairying and cattle raising, for which their training had best fitted them; cheese-making is one of the most important industries. Their settlement has proved a success in every way, by reason of the industry and thrift of the people.

The Crimean War, in 1854, brought many more Swiss to Wisconsin, from Glarus and other cantons, and a large proportion of them settled in Green county. In that county alone, it is claimed, the Swiss now number with their descendants over 8,000 persons, and comprise about a third of the population. Their language is the German-Swiss dialect, which is still used in business affairs. The people belong to the German Reformed faith, which was their religion in Switzerland.

Buffalo county contains a large German element, which is predominantly Swiss. Settlement was begun about 1846–47 by some Germans from Galena, Illinois, who were employed by Capt. D. S. Harris, of that town, to cut wood for the passing steamboats on the Mississippi. Among them was one Swiss family from Graubünden, which is the canton now most largely represented in Buffalo county. They settled at Fountain City (then Holmes's Landing), and were then the only white settlers in that locality. From 1848 to 1855, a few Germans came in each year, and all were engaged in chopping wood. In 1855 the real immigration began; some went by way of Galena, others crossed over from Sauk county, while the rest went directly from Milwaukee by means of ox-teams. The attractions to the Swiss were the excellent soil, the springs of fresh water, and the good pastures, all of which reminded them of their native land. They are located chiefly in townships along the Mississippi River.

In Fond du Lac county, in the town of Ashford, and adjoining it on the south in Washington county, is a group of Swiss who are from the canton of St. Gallen. The first came directly to Wisconsin in the spring of 1847; and between that year and 1856, the majority settled in that locality. They were, with few exceptions, of the peasant class, and here they own farms of from 40 to 160 acres each.

In Sauk county, the towns of Troy, Honey Creek, and Prairie du Sac contain a large Swiss element from the cantons of Graubünden, Zürich, and Bern. They belong to the German Methodist and German Reformed churches.

Among the South Germans in north-central Wisconsin, are also a number of Swiss.

SAXONY.[1]

Among the Wisconsin Germans, there are in almost every community a number of Saxons. In addition to these, Saxon groups have located in Ozaukee, Washington, Sheboygan, and Manitowoc counties. In August, 1839, three Saxon families, possessing considerable means,[2] took up govern-

---

[1] The diversity of conditions in Saxony makes any special account of German life impracticable.

[2] These families were those of Adolph Zimmerman, afterwards member of the State legislature (1870, 1873–74), and two Opitz brothers.

ment land in what is now Ozaukee county. Two or three years later, other Saxons followed them, while still others settled in the town of Mequon, on the old Green Bay road. In September, 1839, seven families, with thirty-six individuals, came from Sax-Altenburg, in the duchy of Saxony, and bought a half section in the same town. Andrew Geitel acted as their leader, and made the purchase.

In Farmington, Washington county, there is a large Saxon element. In 1857, they formed a "Humanitäts Verein" for social, literary, and benevolent purposes. The town contained at one time a German library of 300 or 400 books.

It was probably the influence of Frederick Burchhardt,[1] in Manitowoc, that induced about fifteen families from the vicinity of Kuehmnitz, Saxony, to settle in the town of Mischicott, between 1846 and 1849. A part of the town was, from this fact, called Saxenburg. These people were linen weavers, innkeepers, landed proprietors, etc., but here they became, for the most part, farmers. All members of the group were Lutherans.

In Mosel, Sheboygan county, and Centreville, Manitowoc county, there is a large Saxon settlement, which started about 1847. Its members are from Sachsen-Weimar and Sachsen-Gotha, where they were farm laborers and shepherds; a musical society and Turnverein are supported by them; they are divided between the Lutheran and Catholic churches.

In the towns of Medina, Vinland, Wolf River, and Winneconne, in Winnebago county, there is a scattered Saxon settlement which was formed between 1850 and 1856. Here, the Lutheran faith prevails.

---

[1] Burchhardt was himself a native of Kuehmnitz, and coming to Manitowoc in the early days, rose to a position of prominence.

FROM OTHER STATES.

PENNSYLVANIA GROUP.

In the city of Marathon, there is a German settlement composed of men from Pittsburg.   About 1856, a society known as the "Homestead Verein" was formed by L. W. Koltenbeck, editor of a German republican paper in Pittsburg.   It consisted of about one hundred and twenty-eight members, mostly factory hands and day-laborers, who had recently come over from Würtemberg, Baden, Westphalia, and Bavaria.   They were nearly all Catholics, and as members of the same church were associated in Pittsburg.   That city was crowded, employment was scarce, and they were anxious to better their condition by seeking a home in the West.   Accordingly they sent Koltenbeck and another of their members, a shopkeeper, to look up a suitable place for founding a small village, with farm lands adjoining.   The committee seem to have started without any definite point in view, and probably came to Wisconsin because the Germans were at that time settling here in large numbers.   They chose eight hundred acres in Marathon county, including the site of the present Marathon, which they purchased from a law firm in Stevens Point.   Meanwhile, in the absence of the committee, the society heard glowing reports of land in Minnesota, and, but for Koltenbeck, would have chosen the present site of St. Cloud.   They had also under consideration the city of Appleton, Wisconsin, or some part of Outagamie county. When Koltenbeck returned and announced his purchase, a split occurred in the society, some leaving on account of dissatisfaction over the conditions of the purchase.   The remaining members continued in the society, and sent Valentine Christmann and Joseph Kapp to complete Koltenbeck's purchase.   They were instructed to secure enough more land, so that each member might have 80 acres and three city lots, each one paying for his share $125 in monthly installments.   In the winter of 1856 and

1857, the city was surveyed and platted, and in 1857 the first settlers arrived; among these, the names of eighteen men are still recalled by old settlers. In 1858, the majority of those who were still in Pittsburg packed up and came to Marathon. Bringing some machinery with them, a saw-mill was soon after built, although the dam was not completed until 1869. Since then a grist, a planing, and a second saw-mill have been constructed. The other principal business of the community is farming. Marathon is an exceedingly quiet town, slow but prosperous, and the ruling element is German.

OHIO GROUP.

In the town of Dale, Outagamie county, there is a large group of Germans who came to Wisconsin from Ohio. They were originally from the Rhine provinces and the borders of France, and first settled in Pennsylvania, near Reading. From there they went to Ohio, where they settled in the towns of Richland, Medina, and Ashland, in Columbia county.

In 1853, eight young men from this settlement took their stock and went westward. Six of them became discouraged and remained in Indiana; the other two came to Wisconsin, and located in the town of Dale. Others followed them from Ohio, between the years 1853 and 1855, until about forty families settled in that town. They have grown strong enough to sustain two congregations, one of the Lutheran and the other of the German Reformed faith. They are an intelligent people, and are said to preserve the German spirit and language with much zeal.

CPSIA information can be obtained
at www.ICGtesting.com
Printed in the USA
LVHW021006040121
675397LV00008B/627